Headwaters

Sid Marty

McClelland and Stewart

The Canadian Publishers
McClelland and Stewart Limited
25 Hollinger Road, Toronto

Manufactured in Canada by Webcom Limited

ACKNOWLEDGEMENTS

To Al Purdy for invaluable encouragement
and the Canada Council for a short term grant.

Some of the poems were published previously in
the anthology *Storm Warning,* and in the magazines
Elfin Plot, Vigilante, and *Copperfield.*

Canadian Cataloguing in Publication Data

Marty, Sid, 1944-
  Headwaters

Poems.

ISBN 0-7710-5814-4 bd.   ISBN 0-7710-5807-1 pa.

I. Title.

PS8576.A78H42 1979   C811'.5'4   C74-22415
PR9199.3.M39H42 1979

To Myrna

CONTENTS

DAWN. JINGLIN PONIES

Get up in faint cold light
take some oats in a feed bag
coffee will be ready when I return
mist rising on the Maligne river

Half mile walk to toy horses
motionless in wet buck brush
A light frost that was dew
feet get wet
to where they stand
White mare, the bell mare
shakes her head rings her bell
that Mac found twelve years ago
in distant mountains

In cold light and blue shadow
valley and mountain
their white blazes shine
While gentle mare takes the bit
untie the hobbles on one side
horses crowding round the feed bag
their warm breath on my neck
ride back to camp, geldings following
their mare, ride bareback in the cold air
The mare's warm body
between my wet, chilled knees

SIWASHING   *for Al Purdy*

This is what I would do
if the down timber
stretched to the sky
siwashing, my mind
on a jumping horse
toward a sunset
not only breaking down
but torn away
Riding for the ragged curtain

Is what I do
born fifty years too late
Will not get used to
dying on a cushioned seat
rolling down my grey tomorrows

So I ride these mountains
through the widowmakers
carrying away old snags
that catch on my leather

Had I fringes
I would wear them
all torn up by timber
to flash in the shintangle

Call it 'siwashing'
what we do out here
when we need to go through places
that do not seem desirable

Eye weeping
hat gone
one spur broken
gun butt catching on limbs
half unsaddled
the pony mad, and
flies would eat your socks

And it feels like a saga
so it is
to live your own story
is no lie

It feels strong
it burns the loins
the sun's whiplike motion
through the spruce

Here
is a cliff edge
and
there
is a muskeg hole
there
is the track of a bear

Twist, dodge
turn a useless
half forgotten skill
to service

When the old men all are gone
you must teach it to yourself
and siwashing
that all consuming art
was good enough
for me

EACH MOUNTAIN

Each mountain
its own country
in the way a country
must be
A state of mind

News of the mountains
brought out by the horse guides
long time ago, though some old boys
live long, tell it still in legion halls
how they cut trails to the high tundra
packing a few adventurers
through deadfall of the timber bands
last of the taiga
to find their way
bright with wild cranberry
and flowers

Each mountain
where local climate
controls the shade
of paintbrush and anemone
Colours and moods
vary as the weather, suddenly

But we belonged here too
men and women
our loving squalls
intemperate desires
wide ranging
hot and cold
like August glaciers
as we travelled for pleasure
walking above the trees
and climbing the summits

Because the smell
of wild mountain flowers
of a thousand hues
threatened the civilized monster
carried in us from the highway

Must be tempered
with the threat of loss
Thus we gain
Romantics because
each mountain
made us so
would not have us
any other way

BURNT BY THE TREE

In which sat a small solemn owl
about the size of a baseball
even with my shoulder, riding by

Being watched by some sad heart
I turned, could have touched
But he blinked at the suggestion
in yellow eyed amaze, grey feathered
took his tiny moons off

leaving the tree

Jan. 8 1973

A TWO YEARS CUB

Every night at 10 o'clock
just when I'm nicely dozing off
he climbs my porch
and cuffs with a snort
and a clatter
the white enamel washbasin
like a saucer through the moonlight
yards out into the meadow

I'll be damned if I move that basin
just because it's sitting
on his ancestral trail
bisected by this ancient shack

Listen pup
there's another porch
ten miles up the valley
Why single my sleep out for murder?

Don't laugh!
You come back tomorrow night
gonna boot you up the ass

It's quiet for awhile
I settle down, mollified

Only to shoot up in wild eyed terror

Sounds like a steam engine
nosing through the front door
with two monster firemen
doublehanding coal with steel shovels
and grunting like angry rhinos

Peek out the window. Chagrin.
see a fat bull elk rubbing the velvet
off his antlers on my doorjamb

Enraged, I leaped outside reckless
and hurled a bucket at his head
which missed, and landed among
the grazing horses which stampeded
from the naked madman,

who now sits on his porch
pink skinned, having given up on sleep
to stare at the world revealed by a silver moon

Nov. 1972

DEAD WORDS

Culling flaccid words from language
out of the body of this art
is something like excising
cysts from the lungs of a moose,
spores of the parasite tapeworm
granulosis

Fruits of destruction, apparently harmless
translucent, fluid sun bubbles
(sometimes found big as oranges
in the brain)
camouflaged so perfectly
glibly surrounded
by red tissues of breath

with this difference,
for that exercise makes language sound
while this late surgery
means the animal's death

Feb. 1973
Prince Albert National Park

INSIDE THE MAP   *for Bob Haney*

There is a trail into those ranges
Its continuity more mapped than real
Constantly its aim is cut
by swollen creeks of runoff
Burdened by snowslides
it sags downhill

The dull metal phone line
is lost in a tangle
of trees and mud
The voice fades
shorted through stones
and roots
The twisted line breaks down

The warden there in spring
must cut his way out and in
slashing away half thawed debris
swimming his horses through lonely streams,
salvaging broken packs in the muck

Wet as a rat he rolls a cigarette
thinking to strike the trail on the rockslide
tightening a cinch
longing for fire, his chilled guts
churn for hot coffee
lashed with strong rum

Ten miles, twenty miles
Jaques Lake, Grizzly Shelter
Rocky Forks, and mend corral
shoe horses in the gumbo
Timber wolves howl up the valley
under Mount Balcarres

SHAWN

You're an old horse
furiously willing yourself to die

Today from four in the morning
till midnight
packing the trail crew's food and tents
down from Twin Falls in the rain
It had to be suicide for me
but for your last fibres of restraint
on the black, two foot wide trail
switchbacking down the sidehills,
the two mares biting your flanks
to push us to death or home

Tied nose to tail,
you held them when a halter broke
me with a jackknife sliding
among flying hooves

Carried me down the dark mountain's head
the river a snake, hissing at your heart
iron shoes scraping on stone
in the sparkling darkness

and you're tired of saving my skin

They were glad to see us
the trailcrew, huddled under midnight spruce
by the soggy creek

But at their greeting you reared
the halter strangling, the bit
twisting, cutting your mouth

Your eyes roll wild from the lantern's flame
and the crew grieves for the old man
tearing from light with bloody lips

furiously retreating into night

Montreal, 1969.

AUGUST, THE MOON OF RIPE BERRIES

Late August, and the trail mud
getting harder, the better going
pounded flat by horses and deer
Half asleep in the steep ascent
the thud of hooves rouses me
A brown bear, full of loganberries
rattles the steaming thickets in his course

Duchesnay Lake trail
free of the water now
Pack horse nipping at my wheezing pony

They stiffen, ears up
as a rutting moose charges
knee high through the blue shallows
behind us, a horny juvenile
kicking up rainbows
cooling in Duchesnay water

Rank mooshwa in their nostrils
spooks the horses, I speak softly
dance through a tangle of deadfalls
push in my spurs
The gelding rolls his eye backward
and shows his sage old teeth

He remembers the elbow
in his ribs yesterday
when he stepped on my foot
He still has much to teach me
and I have a lump for each lesson

High water has choked the trail with snags
My last chore in the summer ending
bucking the snags by Duchesnay water

The chainsaw breathes a blue smoke
cool air fills with the roar of the motor
horses sleep on their feet
The bear comes to see them
they are not impressed
runs off when the saw stops, coughing

At the end of the meadow
the lake subsides in a wind
Spruce needles fall from the boughs
where my mare rubs her cheek
on the rough, sticky bark
showering the upturned petals
of the orange paintbrush

The bear returns from his solitary harvest
prowling across my tracks
smelling the ripeness
of big spruce, toppled and broken
three feet thick, promise of beetles
of spruce budworms, like fat white plums

In the quiet now
is the continuous pattering
of ripe fruit falling
on the thick duff
the forest floor

TOAD

Wake up toad it's June
The snow is off your back
Hide under a leaf clumsy legged
Can't you hear coyote coming?
following me up the trail
Can't you feel the sun
on your blistered carapace?

   The snow is gone. Coyote is out hunting
   You sit in his way going   tepwewák   tepwewák

SKID HORSE

Scrawny broken horses
hauling loads of sticks
sheaves of straw
Fat peasants on a market day

Greece and Yugoslavia
Races of old women
with faces glaring
at their stony earth
backs bent from hauling
loads of rock and lumber
running stooped behind
their proud, riding husbands
like whipped dogs

Too poor to starve
a tired horse for work
No horses for skidding
No timber left to skid

Summer of 1971
Tonquin Valley skid horse
name of Rusty
Long haired sway backed rusty gelding
also known as Seldom Swift
but broke for skidding I was told

I clad him in an old sleigh harness
a singletree
chained to some bucked up firewood

The ground was rough
and full of hummocks
the load hung up repeatedly
He got scared and froze
stiff-legged in stubborn mutiny

Winter time's the time for skidding logs

But I climbed aboard, whereat
he charged into the trees
and got stuck in a hole

He and I went round awhile
till I turned him loose
What the hell's the use
while I've got naphtha for the stove
And he's not broke at all for skidding trees
like in that 80's scene

But in Europe now
big clydes ploughing
a Yugoslavian field

Scrawny burros
tied up with us
by a river in Greece
and every animal worth his weight
in gold, that is, meat

and I wrote home

"Man, have you ever heard a burro bray?
On this red wine
I'm sucking up
at 50 cents a litre
You'd bawl yerself to shame
to hear a little brown bugger braying
while packing half a ton of corn shucks
and a fat old bag
clad in black
beating the piss outta him
with a length of cane"

These old women, old horses,
living stooped among thorns
eating the thorns
living

have no choice
but teach their animals
to obey them

BRUSH WOLF

Grin coyote you trickster
lean dog, all teeth and pecker
your fake limp don't fool me

Dog fled from the manger
star gazing coyote
in the long grass of dawn
bouncing up to see me

forked one come to amuse you?
here in a high meadow so far

Bone gnasher, you sly bugger
I'll not frisk with you

For I have seen you rob
the old one of the mountain
Mustahyah, even he!

and chase your tail at the joke

While he plays he's too engrossed
with carrion elk he's rolling in
to fool with pestering coyote

and you play you don't know
he'll make his move
and lope around him grinning

never there when he jumps

Guess he'd have to rub you out
if he ever caught you
But with a certain sadness afterwards

Like a fat old King who buries his jester
and becomes a fool, from want of fooling

Jan. 20 1973

LOW PASS

A man once came this way
and I think I know him
following his blazes
years behind him

A whiteman.
No indian would need
to mark these trees
or look in the water
to recall his face

For in these meadows
he was lonely
It is remembered in silences
that bluebells
hurt him,
and the fields
of blue eyed mary
black eyed susan

A wind
a woman's touch
on his shoulder

Sometimes I lose track
fooled where a bear
blazed a tree
sharpening up
stop,
make a circle
find the right way

Look back, remember
how it looks
then, to his next blaze

moving up,
going on

Long legged filly
she won't stand still
dances in the shadows
among dead limbs

The cinch is tight
she dances
the reins are tangled
the deer flies tease me
and she sounds the air
for wild news

He swings the axe
at a fallen tree

her routines
they bother me
this filly,
dancing
silly
bitch

An iron grey colt
she rolls her eye in shadow
whinnying
And the darkness answers
with half shaped thoughts
left on the wind
that morning
The sky like a letter
edged in black
that the day opened

Blade rings in dead timber
Something . . . but I can't remember

Fearful, circling round the tree
she paws the moss
to get away, get in the clear
But he swings his axe
My business is here

And what does she smell
that animal
carcajou?
grizzly bear?
and that wild wind . . .
but I can't remember

COYOTE RETURNS

Now Seton tells us how coyote
will take to the creek
with a flower in his mouth
lascivious coyote

The yellow one sinks
till just his nose is poking out
the leaf and stem waving around

behind his grin
and then he drops all
to the water
shakes dry, and lopes off
grinning to himself

Crazy Coyote!

yeah. but the leaf, if you look
is covered with struggling vermin

ditched by Meschachakan, the versatile

Jan. 16 1973

THREE BEARS

In early September, yellow light
as snow was falling
and he was alone
returning from woodcutting
plans of putting up wood
for a long winter
In the blizzard without warning
he crossed the silvertip's trail
old sow and cubs, and she charged
out of that swirling light
tearing, tearing him

In the snow he woke up later
(this surmised from the signs found
and she again, feeding nearby
was on him
but seeing no threat
allowed him passage of a kind
under a tree
where he stuffed his sash
a style he wore
into the hole in his side
terrible wound in that cold
and there, he died

2.

In September's fading colours
riding home
three bears, the fatal number
charged the horse which threw him hard
on the downed timber
breaking pelvis and thigh bones
out cold for a time
and coming to, he carved
handholds of sharp stakes
and crawled a mile to his cabin

Piling boxes one on the other
in the intervals of consciousness
he reached the phone
which happened to be working
so they saved him that time

Now he drinks beer in Edson
lives in the old folks home
And they say around the ruin
of that old cabin
there's a bottle of rum he buried
in the roots of an old spruce
But I never could find it

3.

Three weeks passed, and no other voice
but the whiskyjack's mockery round the cabin
I changed my shirt, and rode to Moosehorn Lakes
but the campground was empty

Indian paintbrush flowers
cover the trail
as if rust burst forth in blooms
lulling the senses

I think of Andy Suknaski
baiting a hook with the ochre flower
faithful as a child,
casting it out with a ripple
catching a perfect silver trout
The only fish we caught that day

How we are beguiled

The wind lifts toward the east
to brush these petals
when suddenly, from round a corner
swinging his head from side to side

a Grizzly Bear, silvertip
five, six hundred pounder
coming on so quickly
that motion would be useless

He sounds me, stops at twenty paces
to consider the next move

Speak to this bear
for he may know you,
said a voice
in my frozen senses

So I spoke softly
in his fierce hiatus
a deep and secret language
of love and claws,
a fluency I had only suspected
did make me wonder,
while he reared to his hind legs
in judgement

He swept the air once
with his claws, and hesitated
Dropping to all fours, he grunted
and moving aside
ascended the hill

But I am reminded
I am not at home
Here where I live
only at hazard

There is a darkness
along the bright petals

Oct. 1972

WOLF WILLOW

Wolf willow, muskeg
tree by tree
any faces between
put there by me

Break through in the wildness
burn me!
wash me at the river fords

He made a circle of twenty miles
breaking wolfwillow
to get back home
Twenty miles
a foot at a time

Ground that draws out poison

      civilization

These shadows full of savage nothing
demand fullness

So he sang
all his broken melodies

and as the shadows increased
     he returned
from the mud and the leaves
with one song on his breath
     he returned

MY OWN COUNTRY

Up the long night of Dieppe
floating entranced
with a handful of strange fingers
rode my father
a ghost in a tin hat

Over the broken divisions
in stumbling fire fights
taking their chances
to be done
with the willful impotence
of the previous peace

And over the ocean
through the flotsam wrack
of the late war
sailed my mother
carrying me, a hope
that peace would now be found
in a new land

So I come now
to my own country
to fight a war with myself
for the reach of my body and mind

In my left hand, solitude
and my right casts a fist
too easily
there having been
so many betrayals

For there is a wave
savage parabola
homing from southward
so under these skies,
no news of my people can I hear

This wave invisible
not every man can feel
This wave chafes me
like a band of steel

Only the artless stars
mark my shifting progress
Fathoming the cold, they glitter
impartial eyes of a bestiary

As I beckon with my left hand
and with my right arm, sight them

But in the moment of deciding
just who I am, and what doing
The wave pounds in
against my skull

Yet every night of clear and cold
I try, and try again
to hold what I am standing in

For now I am come to my own country

IN THE MOON OF FROZEN LEAVES

In a blue roomed cabin
beset by news
of a wild winter
and the toiling wars
I sit
and plot the conduct of
a single day

The quarrelsome wind assaults
rebounds
dealing snow at every shuffle
round the house

Soon the avalanche must roll
down its accustomed paths
where only alder bushes grow

long forecast
by the shifting view
of rocks, of wars

that all must end
with gravity and power
here in this wintry hour
and without, in the flowering cold

Nov. 1972
Miette Cabin
Jasper Park

PORTENTS OF SPRING

Bashing through the crusty drifts
like a winded moose pursued by wolves
breaking trail up Lofthouse Creek
to mobilize my life against this cold

Through rattling cattails I smelled
the water, rotten underneath the ice
and stopped, not wanting
to be let down in it
with the long Cree snowshoes on

But the ice is sound
the wind is blowing down my throat
from an old beaver dam

In his round hutch on the slough
Amisk hoots once
when he hears me at the airhole
small pipe of ice

Warm air rises to the finger tips
A stir of furry bodies seems
a gangbang of beavers down below

I shout   "hello. what prophecies
of an early breakup"

Silence.   and a good stink
of sulphur and of poplar shoots

This scent drifts on the ice
in the odourless winter
from the ice chimney

Smell of the patient, fertile muck
watched over by Amisk
through the long night

Jan. 22 1973

COYOTE'S FEAST

Coyote was waiting on the road
where blood and packed snow
led to the moose kill

Coyote had been feeding when he heard
the truck coming, and skulked out
to see this traveller
and what he would do

I sat and looked at coyote
on his haunches, grinning
stupid dog. I could be a trapper
native hunter, triggerhappy rancher

Why do you always think
you know it's me

Sat and looked at coyote
till he looked away, and started
back toward the kill, which was fresh
still steaming, smelled it walking in
behind coyote, who turned downwind to watch

Head, hide, paunch of a cow moose
nose left on
Don't think the Crees done this
hunting at night, beer bottles
on the road for miles
Likely a whiteman poaching here
but you never know

Find the uterus. there it is
a circle of skin burned into the snow
warm barrel of blood

Opened my knife and made a long cut

Head borne on the dark waters
foetus slid dead into my bare hands

Walking back to the road
I met coyote coming back in his circle   *Feb. 13 1973*

FOX ON THE WIRE

Where did you come from
red one
to dance upended
deadly still
on barbed wire
in the south country
of Saskatchewan

A herd of deer
run the edge
of yellow stubble
All around
the purple crocuses
stretch to the Wood Mountain
over spring wet earth

Here on the nuisance ground
flowers bedeck a rusty ford
old cans full of sweet water
hold the sky, mirror your body

Your coat was prime and full
soft as new snow, red like autumn fire

MEAT IN THE SNOW

Nothing moves this winter morning
and that is recorded by the pitched ears
of wolf and deer,
nothing moving

Then an engine rumbles
a truck drifts through
the long aisle of Jackpine

Now does this driver
give some meaning
to the mute sweep
of winter bush?

no

There is meat in the snow
The land only poises
waiting for its discovery
by the wheeling ravens
hung like flags in the grey sky

As for me, I am irrelevant
unless I disturb the sphere
of these dependencies
or fall into the cycle
of raven and wolf

But I will do neither
Because I say
that I give meaning here
despite my bloody prospect
out of arrogance,
or the tears of my realized nullity

I will make something else
out of meat in the snow
to raise the failing argument
we wage with death

I will make something else

a poetry
to ease the racing heart   *Jan. 1973*

EASTER HIGHWAY

All of Canada
stirring awake
with cars like bright cells
on blue veins of a map

And I believe
our heritage
riven by Sun's path
And wived to the westward road

The moving mountains
are well punched
though they pound themselves below

Dynamite cut daylight to their hearts
Through granite wounds man goes

And I think these drivers
are good and evil
on missions of love,
or clumsy murder

Of that
naivete is the measure,
though distance divides motive

Below evergreen
woven hills
dusted in snow

We are not going
with horses
and harness bells
on winter sleds

But in the wake
of these old dreams

Our history was ploughed
by icehung mountains
through the trailing clouds

THE PUMP

Summer came, and the hazard high
A call came through
for the knuckle busting
firepump
that failed us once

This air is smoke
Sundown, fire
are the same
in the great hurting forests
no man now will claim

So, breathing smoke
I stripped the valve
to mend its fault

Out fell a desiccated mouse
nest and all
in his buff coat
from the shiny centre

Oats and poison seeds
brimmed at his throat,
but our trap
was a hard bargain

For, nested in steel ventricle
his chest heaved tight
and blocked the engine

His rigour spread, a terror
of men running from the fire

As I, with sweat burning these cuts
inhale ashes, taught to stand
dried out frame of the heart
in my hand

YELLOWHEAD

What's written is little, so argues me a fragment
of the past, fair haired trapper of the smoky peaks
gave my name to the famous pass, and Tete Jaune Cache
I had a name once, now I am Yellowhead

Now that I'm a place and not a man
my faults are forgotten, why should I remind you

History magnifies everything

Like others, I was all flash and fire once
a young buck in tight breeches
My head was an emblem, and protean
I managed to keep it on my shoulders
No mean feat in the times I lived in

I tell you this
It was a hard life

So you built your highway
and stole my emblem
my brave belt don't fit you
so bask in secondhand magic
and buy off the dead as long as you can

I could not keep a secret
keep my power hidden

Everywhere I went they knew me
a bright flame
moving through purple shadows

They said   it is Tete Jaune
it is Yellowhead,

Yellowhead

Jan. 1973

HAY MEADOW CREEK

Many horses die in winter range
on Hay Meadow Creek
under the shadow of Devil's Head mountain
Ranges of the eastern wall
mark their bones, where clear water
flows through the white frames

Fishing for brook trout
we heard the wetlands beat
to the hooves of half wild horses
Brewster's wrangler in buckskin
chases ponies weary of dudes
desiring only to join the wildies
take their chances with weather, run free

Told us the grass was scarce
the snow deep
Old horses get weak going for water
get down, can't move
and wearily drown

Fishing for trout among clean bones
where a beaver swam out
Muskrat lived in his round house
A day of sunshine, hail, then rain

At night we baked fish
The coyotes, hearing the dog bark
howled, surrounding our camp
Out there they look in
seeing fire's red star
Their voices suspended
ride the flat, cold air
driving the dog mad
out of the firelight
We caught him in the timber
shut him in the truck

First star over the Devil's Head
The coyotes, running in circles
bark for joy
since clear nights promise a late snow

Out on the old horse graveyard
the last trout jumps
and the ripple
fades into blackness
goes out

PACKING DYNAMITE

"Th thing to remember"
he said
bull durham bag suspended
archly from one pinky
"is to keep your dynamite
and your blasting caps
in two separate places"

Caps were in the saddle bags
dynamite on the mare
and back and forth my horses
battled for the lead
banging packbox and saddle
roughly together
eight miles up the river
to the camp above Twin Falls

My sun tan flaked off
and I was a white and shining angel
ready to take wing
all in white pieces
of a horse shit bomb

THE WORK OF HANDS

Making a pot of coffee
with cold spring water
Splitting the winter's wood
with precise strokes
of a heavy headed axe
keeps the mind fixed
for a time, on work
and stills the ache of love
that quickens to
the transitory flutterings
of violet butterflies
in green grass
Showers of petals
wavering in the sun
with their touch
like stricken notes
of silent music

Enjoining the mind
to the work of hands
Rubbing oil in leather rigging
Busting knuckles shoeing the gelding
Enforcing rhythms, coloured with blood

Yet still intrude
those flashing counterpoints

the sparrow hawk
killing in the sedge,
and sudden evening of the trees

Words from my lover
lightly written
in this book
Love made cruel by distance

Then intention fails
the rope won't splice
as hand falters in mid trade
from heavy clay, its craft
its life

Aug. 1972
Miette Cabin

42

FIRE ON THE RAILWAY

Fire on the railway!
burning up the national dream again

Hot spark from a boxcar's brake
hit the oily speeder ramp
Black smoke rising

  (and this month
   the porcupine
   rattles like death
   the dry leaves
   Shakes his dusty quills
   Cinder mouth on flinty ground

   Through the brown grass
       gunpowder
   running up hill, the
   watercan bangs
   on ribs each lunge
       breathless
   and work fire to death

   Fire up and dancing
   like an old red flag
   falls on the orange ties
   to pick up strength

   Enviously beat it
   into hot soupy muck
   Stir it with the shovel
   Feel for it
   with your hands

TH POCOHONTAS KID

Th Pocohontas Kid
was the handle, hung
on a young warden
in Pocohontas district

A palpable title
as the kid's voice
quivering on the radio was
"Worried about a flat tire"
they said, "or some knothead
five minutes late
from a mountain climb"

The kid's voice
giving off bad vibrations
amid the silence of the pine
and heat waves
smoke of forest fires
distant, and too terrible
to contemplate

His tenor, rising a pitch
could bring tears of commiseration
"th sad son-of-a-bitch"
they might say, looking off
to distant hazy vistas
to fire lookouts
choking blind in smoke
impotent

Wishing they could
turn off the radio
"Jesus Christ"
they would swear softly
in the midst
of shoeing a horse

Swatting huge
steak eating flies
amid horse farts
"Jesus Christ"
they would say
The kid's voice echoing
in a distant truck

ABBOT

So they've named a pass for me
and built a hut there
Well why not
I died well, I fell off a mountain
the first attempt on Mount Lefroy

I was going to see new places
to foot the ridgepole of the continent
off balanced I guess
by the completely indifferent climate
That kind of clearness in the air
makes men dizzy

Others have fallen since
Dead men have been left
in Abbot's Hut for safekeeping
overnight, like the one Fruhman
the guide offered tea to, arriving
in the night, he thought the bunkrooms
must be full, and this sound sleeper
on the kitchen floor had no bed
bundled in his sleeping bag

But there's many stories of that place

Men fall off mountains because
they have no business being there
That's why they go, that's why they die

WHEN IT RAINED

When it rained
sky's belly slashed
by sheet lightning
burst
let roar the soft water
into the lakes
and the lakes rose higher

Washed a road off the mountain
with big boulders potting the cars
and the pilgrims cried out to us
for towing chains and bandaids
comforts in a whirlwind rain

Sloppy hillsides
slumped into the water
rising to meet the rain halfway

Canada geese in formation
steamed through the front yard
of my cabin, the stew pot
floated out with a load on
Swim for your dinner
said I to the mirror

and beheld
th Pocahontas Kid afloat
in cowboy boots
His spurs flashed in the foam
a fighting, scalded rooster

Rained on his head
and his blood cooled
till only his eyes out there
glow in the dark, weeping night

floating west to the drowned sunset

"I do suspicion" said he,
"that it's goin' t' rain"

THE FIRES

Up on the edge of the burnt out timber
lightning struck twice after many years
come back to finish the job
up Chaba Creek

That summer it seemed the whole country
was on fire, smoke blew down from Grande Cache
eighty miles, and sank in every valley
Out in the bush, you knocked on wood and prayed
to be saved from fighting fire

As the temperature rose, day by day
more inevitable, you started seeing fires
everywhere, nervous reports crackled
over the radio, until you wished
the thing would come and be done with
tired of being teased, playing mouse
to the gigantic pleasures of the sun

Damned if it didn't come, all in a lump
three fires. The first we put out in a few days

then raised our heads, and holy jesus!
there was another one
funnelling out of a hanging valley
little known peak named Quincy
ready to round a high corner at 75 hundred
and blow down on the Athabaska

Down in Jasper they've got their own fire going
a showpiece fire above the town
The penpushers are building careers on it
They don't want to meet its big brother

1. *The Chaba Fire*

By eight o'clock we flew in to set up camp
My crew were all draft dodgers, volunteers
looking sad on the army whirlybird

The Air Element so called
dropped us on an island in the river
freaked us out most bitterly,
our amphibious assault

Poor dodgers suffered for their bread that night
pitch black, all of us naked
formed a line in the glacial water
balancing ten gallon drums, tents, fire pumps
up to our balls two hours, nearly swept away
by the strong current, and moving rocks
of the Athabaska, near its headwaters
the Columbia Ice Fields

One man sank in a hole with a tent
on his head, shouted "it's alright I can swim!"
but when he tried, he couldn't move his arms
and was fished out by the hair, the best handle

We stumbled into camp nearing dark
A boy of seventeen was building coffee
in a bucket, was made bullcook on the spot
We expected miracles that night
none of us was even armed with matches
but we had fire enough nearby
banked, and moving toward us in the blackness

Men swinging clumsy grub hoes
wore their way through tough green trees
they couldn't see, swung wildly at nothing
and set up twelve man tents by touch
in their various semicomatose conditions

The boss flew in on the last stick
and looked around on an island so forlorn
confronted by struggling naked men
linked arm in arm in the leaden water
ghostly white in the light of the stars

and waded proudly across with his clothes on
said "Haven't you got the camp set up you dinks"

But that fire was the least of our troubles
we put it out in three days
and the men stood around laughing
thinking of all the grass and granola
they could buy with their overtime
making plans for the road

Smiles saying ok what else
can you show me

That's when the lightning strike hit Mount Quincy

2. *The Quincy Fire*

That hanging valley held a lake
fed by its own glacier
A world where man had never stepped
frequented by goats, birds
and a few hardy squirrels

The helicopter dumped us out upon a rock slide
We scrambled through a maze of quartzite
creek fords and shintangle to the fire edge
Each man shouldering his load as best he can
All being strangers, this is a hard thing
Most owed no allegiance to the Government's plan
But for their money than, they hold the bargain
and all came in at last

We built a landing ramp beside the lake
cut off by cliffs, the air our sole escape
One chainsaw man of talent
trained young men on the spot
an old time timberman, priceless
on a fireline, and rarer every year to find
this trade made obsolete too soon

The way the fire spread was this:

The strike hit in overaged spruce
long past its prime and rich with sap
trembling in the heat, long due

Fanned by wind the trees candled
like blocks of paraffin
Heat sucked water into steam
and scalded the nozzlemen, drove them
crying and cursing like pygmies before it

Fire marched until it hit the rockslide
an avalanche slope, up which we hacked
our fireline through gravelly earth and alders

We pumped in relays water from the lake below
lungs like ash from dragging hose
up and down the slopes
that seemed near vertical

But updrafts carried fire
to the summit cliffs of Quincy
A few trees there began to burn
we watched baffled

Then the first logs blazing
came crashing down upon us
to fall behind our fire line
and drive us into desperate effort

impossible. for fire now was in the rocks
where duff had sifted many yards
in layers of the ancient slides
Now fire was tunnelling underfoot
and shooting overhead

So after that we tried a different plan

Two crews pinched the fire from below
while ours was flown out front
high above, to hold the fire
at its last corner

The landing pad was on a precipice
we set down there like a bird on a perch
In taking off, the pilot dropped straight down
to pick up speed, and make your gorge rise

There was a tarn set by that lip
from which we pumped water
uphill to a relay tank
then half a mile across Mount Quincy
above treeline, downhill to the fire
through the steep meadows of cinquefoil
and heather, but still
we barely pumped enough
to fill our gieke cans
that each man packed
But we caught the fire with our hands
one morning, when it was weak
and strangled it

With a lot of help from the wind
blowing strong down our necks

This turned the fire in against itself
and drove it to the headwall ice
killed it with indifferent cold

So the mountains decided without us
not to burn out the Athabaska valley
destroy the scenery, and bankrupt
the Chamber of Commerce incidentally
while widening the watersheds
in a blaze of fireweed magenta

And after the last tools were picked up
still warm in the ashes, and the crew
taking a final bath in the Athabaska,
that's when the prayed for cumulus appeared
damned if it didn't pour down rain

BEAR AGAIN

Muskwa came up the trail behind us
from the Ottertail
He wanted to rob our lunch

Jerry tried to bluff him with the chainsaw
he put his hackles up
meaning   screw off. I want those goodies

It was a standoff until the chainsaw
choked up, water in the gas

I tried to grab the rucksack
in the silence that followed,
but bear had his paw in first
and fixed me with a red eyeball
stared me down
most bitterly

Mine like two pissholes in a snowdrift
from boozing late the night before
lacked credibility I guess

"I'm hungry bear," I whispered
I was stating a fact merely
as he fished out the bags
with his dainty meathooks

Tough titty quoth he, or would have

and scoffed the whole works
wax paper and all
before our famished eyes

as Jerry got the saw going
and chased the little bugger
down the trail,
and him grinning all the way

THE CUT

My sutured riding boot
I sewed with fishing line
day we rode into Jacques Lake

Scapel fine
as though I'd been honing
a blade for my own limb

Thinking of days gone
with a small saddle axe
whittling a big fir stump down
for firewood

Thinking of the trip to come
dangers of sidehills in the rain
being crowded off the bank
by spooked up ponies
to fall helpless into a river
or rounding blind corners
to meet dead end grizzlies

and lost the present moment
the actual
It glanced down in full swing

An icy sliver kissed my thought
into a pained shout

I woke up the blood in my shoes
and cannot remember
how the dreams turned out

THROWING THE DIAMOND

Throwing the diamond
for the first time
though only on a dummy horse
built of a rusty barrel
held up by hay wire
to four pines

A pack saddle, pack baskets
and for a top pack
the box from the Moose's salt lick
while he stands back there
dumbfounded, but austere
the Great Canadian Fable, unsung

Yesterday, I felt
about as useful
as tits on a stallion
while Bob packed
three horses singlehanded
(not bad for the space age)
jumped in the saddle
and cocking his hat
rode away to the Rocky River

But today I've learned
that shaman knot
that makes a horse
jump logs and cliffs
to follow you anywhere
once it's tied
Knowing he needs you
to loosen the ropes
Cause he'll buck and sunfish
but the load stays on
with a well tied diamond

"Three horses" said Mac
"is nothin. why I've packed
twenty head and more alone

They'd follow me anywhere once tied
up and down mountainsides
on the geographical survey,
through muskeg up to their arseholes

And there's seven kinds of a diamond
I've shown you the easiest only. . . .
But this here haywire horse you've tamed
must be
about the meanest sonofabitch
I ever did see"

MALIGNE LAKE POEM

Dull sky at morning
I walked to the mouth
of the canyon
thinking of you
of fire and water

as the dawn came up like that
over the log boom
angry red on a mean river
trapping the spring adrift

Fishing, I caught no fish
Empty, walked home
wet from the cold dew

May begins without you
the east where you lie
is at dawn on fire

Here there is only the water
in the shadow of Mount Leah

CHAINSAW MAN

Brown in the evening
Hacking
jerking
keeping the boys awake

  "For chrise sake
    you auld bastard
    Give up and die"

Brown in the morning
clad in rusty long johns
Pulling out an oily
flannel shirt
Puts it on

Hacking
coughing
in his coffee
Grizzled beard steamed
by the warm cup

Brown with the chainsaw
can drop it on a dime
    quick as he bucks 'em up

Falling the spruce
    Hacking
The chainsaw
howling
drowns him in sound

Falling the larch
boots in the juniper
spitting snoose

July
The resins intoxicate
The conifer scent
rich with sun

He is falling a Douglas fir
then the dead snags topple
with the long needled pine

The spruce stand steel colour
in dew crystals
of hammered mica

The lodgepole pine
like greenfire
refracts the sun

Brown in the sun
heather hot around his legs
Stores it gratefully
in his cold old age

Brown is sixty-five
and perhaps tubercular

He is the chainsaw man
skilful
at falling the conifer

He is falling

TOO HOT TO SLEEP

He was sleeping when bear
came down from the mountain
by the water trap
after cleaning the screen
of branches and gravel

He fell asleep, a hot june morning
above Wapta Lake, the Kicking Horse Pass
When Muskwa came down without a sound
and snuffed at his jeans

Who's this asleep on my mountain?

It's my friend Birnie asleep I said
(in my head
I didn't hear you coming bear
I was dozing, I looked up
and there you were

You never know said Bear
just where the wind will lead me
when I'll be around
or what beat I'm hunting on

and sniffed at Birnie's collar
at his ear, which he licked tentatively
causing Birnie to moan softly

Nothing doing here he said, nothing doing

"We were just going bear," I said quietly
edging backwards

Don't move too quickly will you, said Bear
when you move, or better still
don't move at all

Are you here often, are you coming again?
he asked, flipping over a stone
licking delicately the underside
"No," I said. good he said, that's good.

I just came down from the pass
the wind blowing up my nose
to see who was sleeping on my mountain
he said, and sniffed at Birnie's armpit
Whoosh   whoosh he snorted

and turned away, clattered down the creek
popping his teeth, his hackles up
Went out of sight
around the shoulder of Mount Hector

as Birnie woke up rubbing his eyes
"Too hot to sleep he said." Yeah.

LITURGY FOR A DEAD FUEL PUMP

Ken is trying to tell me something
over the roar of the diesel generator
his face magnified by the white bulb
I'm holding up, frozen by noise

Straining to get his pulverized speech
His mouth contorts, shooting the words
into a chaotic vacuum, I try
to understand

Why is it
we can't open the door
step out of this painful room
into the 40 below silent spruce bush
that bends down to weigh each syllable

and bury the ghost of the dead fuel pump
he holds so tenderly in his battered hand
steaming in the 90 degree indoor racket

The cycle meter spins up, off the dial
Voltage shoots up and the light pops out

In the darkness, in the pulsing roar
he leans over the naked engine
Radiator blades whirl by his tired flesh
Silver tools fill his searching hands

Jan. 17 1973

BY THE GREAT MAJESTIC

Ninety-eight cents for a hundred pounds of coal
I bagged it myself, drove it on the scale
Litite coal, coal from the mines of mountain towns
with names like Coleman, Canmore, Michel
Where they sit dirty in the beer parlour
after work, coughing in their beer
talking of the tragedies of lay-offs

Old forgotten names like Luscar
on the Coal Branch
Mountain Park, Anthracite
abandoned places
remembered mainly
for their pitiful cemeteries
blackened crosses, shacks of the '30s

Coal hacked from the dreams of dead men
like the kid I went to school with
Brilliant miner's son
the pride of his family
who died in a cavein
like seven men killed
in four short years
in the Grande Cache mine
digging coal for the Japanese mills
for American profit, the Kaiser monolith
all these deaths subsidized by Alberta government

Ninety-eight cents for a hundred pounds of coal
dirt cheap
Shovel it in a burlap bag
pack it in the stove

sixty year old iron from a prairie farm
named "The Great Majestic" made
in Louisville, Kentucky
as I sit out an easter blizzard
in this summer cottage
safe and warm for now
while the coal holds out

while in Michel, the shift goes in
into the deep, dark ground

GRUB HOE

Chunk of the grub hoe
slashes white roots
red soil
Thunk in old orange fibres
of blowdowns
buried deep in dead spruce needles

Chunk. down in this job
sore back, sore arms
blistered fingers bleed

Building a trail
six inches at a swing
so slowly, it fills in behind me
for foot of man to follow
a planned, irrevocable course

egged on by the snoose chewing foreman
heavy booted logger from Sicamous

Clunk goes the blade striking quartzite
Brief sparks do not light a darkness
into which all routes vanish

Thunk goes the blade anyway

Paying my dues six inches at a swing
The body remembers
the long tunnelling darkness
and light seen briefly at the end

Jan. 1973

SASKATCHEWAN CROSSING CAFE

Mountains are unmoved by music
everything that money can buy
fails, where they lean in the window

I got spurs
that jingle
         jangle
    jingle

but broke them on stones

I work around here
but everything I blast
or smash
is healed by running water

Moss grows back
like a green flesh
Tree stumps rot
and disappear

The jangling steel guitar
the radio bonging away
are stifled out there
in the sound
of falling water
falling ice
falling rock
falling snow

And the music
breaks down

TOBY

Got a picture of you
with my arm around your neck
and you dejected
it being a heavy arm
and a heavy ass
to lug around the mountain sides
of Tonquin Valley

Guess I worked you pretty hard
that last month, when the snow
was getting deep
Scared you a few times too
crossing slides of rocks
and corrugated ice

Looking for the angry grizzly sow
Who'd treed two hikers in the Tonquin Valley
and happy not to find her too
we were
I was glad to be on a horse
one with a good nose, and strong legs
like yours
and a bear could hear or smell you
farting miles away

In a letter they tell me
now you are dead
with seventeen horses
all lost
The fever killed you

And I recall your trembling legs
and that you needed to be shod
that last day
But I was anxious
to get out of the cold
said goodbye, for that year
in the muddy corral

So I write these tear jerker lines
An animal I worked with
depended on
and was my friend
from depending
on me

ON BEING SPREAD THIN   *for Barry*

Wear on crippled speech
sway backed verbs creaking

tired of working, tired of speaking
Collapsing after 8 hours of labour
a beast brought to earth

and awake chained to a desk
to try and make magic, write poems

Decking out the same sad tree
with its load of crows
Jacking up the sun's red winter
with fractured treble clefs

Scribble scribble scribble eh
another damned book eh

Art, said the poet
is so easy to give up

What's worse
went and bought a red mustang car
and drove through the cold mountains
with tears in his eyes

Dec. 20 1972

"What is Swamp Fever you ast?
Well I would 'splain it this way
young feller

Spose I took and put straw
in a bucket of water
And was to take and put
yer foot, left or right
makes no matter
in that same pail
and leave you settin'
few days in that water

Nails would curl up, turn black
foot would swell
your knee would swell
and your body fill with poison
from the germs in the rotten mixture

Take yer horse that catches fever
from runnin on wet ground
and stagnant waters
Many days he's been there prowlin'

You gotta knife? you gotta pen?
ok I got pen. see this pen?
nice pen eh. (Jesus, where's that waiter).

Well you ever feel a horse's hoof boy?
Sure is hard ain't it
if you evered had a horseshoe
labelled on your ass,
you'd know how hard it is

but you take this pen
to a horse with swamp fever
an you could drive it in
the softened hoof right out of sight
so there's yer diagnosis

Now what can you do for such a fever?
First, the swelling must be below the knee
If above, your only cure
is a high-powered rifle
coz that's what they call
a poor prognosis

But if it be below the knee
You must get that horse down
tie him down
in his fever

But first you gotta make yer poletice
outta anything you got
but especially outta bran and onions
But also outta old bread and onions
the older the better
or chop an onions, any kind
Wheat chop, oat chop, corn
or porkchop, ground into paste
with big spanish onions
like grandma's gruel
to draw the poison

Then you take a sharp knife
and lance that horse from knee to ankle
not in the muscle, between the bones

Then grab your nose
coz if you ever smelled a nuisance ground
that's the smell of swamp fever

But slap that poletice on his wounds
and keep him down, keep him down
in his fever

an WAITER
bring another round
for my friend here"

Mar. 1972
Calgary

FOR YOUNG MEN

He said it was for young men
young men and fools
the rescue team

To be caught on the wrong side
of creeks or crevasses
when the temperature will change
world falls round your ears,
"and I don't like the knothead
what's ramroddin'
that outfit"
His way of making it plain,
"You won't catch me
on no goddam mountain"

There's many more
would speak the same
all worn out
with easeful death

As smelling out
some lost highjumper
searching on the glacier
they find him. spread
for the picking up
Them risking their necks
to witness his adventure

The ravens worked to change
the darkening, empty head
"Sure is open minded"
one of them said
His way of numbing the pain

BRIGHT MORNING

The baby's hairbrush, blue handle
soft silver bristles
rests in the window
on a box of bullets
The fine print reads
"308 cal. soft nosed
180 grams" in this bilingual land
"Balle a extrémité emoussée"

I shoot that rifle
makes a helluva noise
that leaves the silence terrified
But can't drown out a railroad
or a mother's cry

I love the mountains

From the window
they are silver maned
posed, resolute
Wind combs them

I brush the baby's hair
he loves the red label
on a jar of nivea cream

Summer 1972

AMONG THE DROWNING SINGERS

Among the drowning singers
I remain
now isolate upon a stone
observe the diving bird
flash through sky and cooler zones
of water
flatbill popping in the air
to sing his twonote
raucous tune
that keeps me wired here
by anchor bone

In my pack a deer's white jaw
which, when sun breaks in the grey
I will wave at the speeders
on the Jasper highway

It was killed by wolves
in a cold month
my amulet
against the deadly lanes

Was found high in the timber
where no man's been
charmed by a loon
who cried
when I touched the bone
down on the lake below

And over the drowned singers
their hair twisting
flamboyant lines
the pines sigh in elegy
and Coyote too sings
laughing, in low water August

When they emerge
their smiles eclipse the glaciers
into momentary darkness

To the cry of a blackbird
the wind changes seasons

They sink again under snow
Their charm wears off,
their pure white style remains

SASKATCHEWAN AND THE ROCKY MOUNTAINS (1859-1860)

Southesk, casually lighting your meerschaum
and sparking a prairie fire
covering thousands of acres
you said "the conflagration
raged far and wide. I never heard
to what extent it spread. . . . "

How I loved your wanton naïveté
the things you left unsaid
lest you be undone
in literary circles

Your notes on Shakespeare
made while icicles ran
down your nose in a winter tent

Your trigger happy aspirations
somehow at odds with your careful study
of the prairie chicken *Tetrao Cupido*
(your etymology), now nearly extinct
alas, along with the buffalo grass

and the English aristocracy

Dec. 1972

MERCY

I killed a wapiti
heavy and female
with sledgehammer shots
that drove blood and sense
down on its knees

Mauled by dogs
she took to the river
and lost her fawn
over the falls

trapped by water
and cliffs, dying slowly
and I released her
waited for the knowledge
to appease me

Dogs and men have the world
and they worry it to death
running, grinning
Here is the dog
with blood in his mouth
and the gun still warm in my hands

Dogsoldier, tell me
Is man like a deer
you sight through trees,
lost in the wars
trapped by hazard
A fear you tear out
release him, bleeding

And who do you meet
in your lurid dreams
If your sleep is troubled
as mine,
smiling soldier

Is life but a shit
and a tramp through mud,
and for motto this:
if you can't eat it
or screw it,
piss on it

If you see what I mean
I thought life in this park
should be holy
and no killing
would be at random

You've been too long
with the masters of war
and so, farewell

I put myself above the rapids
looked into the doe's eyes
We heard our pulses
threw hearts before us
I slammed home the bolt
sent her to wind's chorus

THE ARGUMENT FOR ASCENDING

Sidehill gouging
gives your ankles pain
stiffkneed evenings
and arthritic old age

Slabrock and ice
have let so many down
from an awkward balance
to their finger ends
The mystery of falling

Gravity too, is my domain
It turns you, swimmer, over
I watch from the steep approaches

Would you be the man for the mountain?
The skulls of goats, the skulls of sheep
foot my precipitous fences

Learn to fail sometimes, bear with me

Your body is the cross you carry
up to the high places

And your reward
a tearing wind
a view

of endless higher mountains

A SEARCH

Turns out the man with epilepsy
did not die alone up Meadow Creek
but having missed the trail completely,
he crawled over a mountain range
and came down on the highway
near Dominion Prairie

And turns out the man I tracked
down Meadow Creek in the rain
horse attempting to present me
with close ups of muddy terra
was just some phantom fisherman
or wild spook wandering
crazy through the greenery

But I did meet a wrangler
when night fell
who'd ridden in from Jasper
and we exchanged opinions
on lost horses and fools
near Maccarib pass
and the grave of a warden
killed by a grizzly in 1929

While the moon shone
through a mist of fine snow falling
on the antlers of a deer by the water
on two lovers alone by a fire
and on me, riding five miles
over wet shining stones
horse's bells shivering
over the meadows

Sept. 1971
Tonquin Valley

THE MAD MOUNTAINEER

When J. thought he must be abandoned
at the end of the lake
left to the long night of the mind
after his day of mad mountaineering
solo climbing on the glaciers
He got a bushy notion
to build himself a cosy
squirrel nest, there
on that wild shore of Maligne
by the cruel water

And instead of building a fire
in the big stone circle
to keep his phantoms at bay
He built his bed of moss
on the cold ashes
with walls of firewood
roofed with branches
of spruce and tamarack
just big enough to squat in
curled up like Job
in his ash pile

Such a spooky thing to come upon
J.'s legacy
when the boat returned
and took him off unexpectedly

"What the hell's that?"
mac yelled
"goddamdest wicki-up I ever seen"
as we tore it down
restoring the logs to their pile
the moss to the forest
of more logical forms

while on the stern
of a disappearing boat
J.'s arm flapped farewell

"Yeah goodbye" yelled Mac
"see ya in the funny papers"
and added

"I guess now we can go home
and shoot ourselves,
because now
we've seen everything"

2.

Still climbing alone
J.'s latest stunt
Three boys on the timber crew
heard him going up
cliffbands of a steep ravine
shouting constantly GERONIMO!
kicking down boulders
avalanching
all the way

"Are you alright?"
"course I'm alright"
he yodelled, BANZAI!
Stuff still whistling down
when I arrived, big slabs
falling a thousand feet
end over end, a fluttering sound
like idling propellers
then smashing in the canyon
releasing a sulpherous stink
from the ancient rocks shattering
in bursts of dust

Why I worry about you
I don't know
Mountain rescue is great
for the rescuee

But now I have a pretty young wife
I become partial to Mac's
untested theory

"can bring any crazy bastard down
with a 270"

URBAN PERILS

Twenty-four days in the back country
cut off by a stone curtain
living dangerously alone
and careful, to avoid accidents

A horse fell on me twice
and I was unscathed
kicked at me and she missed

falling repeatedly on the muddy trails
the slippery gooseshit

flew once over a small cliff
some fifteen feet
and landed absurdly in an aspen
hung up like a soggy owl

so blithely, under the heavens

Travelled the rough country
swamping trails with axe and chainsaw
splitting wood each day

On my day off I got drunk in Banff
all unwittingly at A.P.'s party

And in the dark it was
climbing that primrose path
to the Art School
with Jack the painter
formerly of the Hamilton Tiger Cats

I slipped and fell down on a stump
and broke, incredulous, two ribs

NIGHT CAMP BELOW MALIGNE PASS

Standing in the dark meadow
drinking coffee
The white bell mare
in mountain shadow
her bell clinking
a cold night in
The stars
vastly
shine in the metal
A tame bull moose
wades through willow

Campfire lights up the tent
Woman throws a branch
upon the fire
On the trail
is the five-toed
track of a grizzly
"our brother across the river"
Horses think of 'mustahya'*
and of getting by me
Though they're hobbled
they've learned
to jump
their front feet
down the trail
to home

*Cree word for "mighty bear"

ON HIGHWAY 16, JASPER

Leaving the swamp at night
the moose was a dark cloud
floating in mist, to cross the road

Lights stopped him, hypnotized
and the first car caught him hard
in his creaking back legs

Half thrown, half lunging
fell in a spray of glass
his hocks torn open
An animal never pushed that hard before
got up and fell into the ditch
to the water there, safe element

Trailing one shattered leg
learning all in a moment
in acceptance, how obvious
the death dealing highway is

as the trail of a wolverine, a stink
that deer avoid
the look and smell of it
signifying death

Moosewa swam to a willow thicket
catching his useless leg on a snag
he found the dark centre of pain
and trembled

Next day drove him further in
struggling wild as the deer flies
clumped on his wounds and fed

the sun a swollen burr in his skull
whose brittle pricks jarred each nerve,
the red sky eclipses
to a black moon

Silence now. my place is to move
in the arms of water
driving the fish before me
to the heron
feeding as I do
deep in a green well
of silence

I dreamt I was a fish with legs
and the heron had one in his bill
tearing me into the sky
silently
for I had no voice

Sun went out in the lake
three times, while he circled
followed by coyote
licking blood
from the pine needles

So appearing at the road again
the dim division of his range
that cut him from himself

There he fell for the last time
slowly, rolling backward to the swamp
he sank, his eyes wide and brown
as the murky bottom

Coyote abandoned him then
taking the road at a dead run
into the safety of the far trees

Summer, 1971

DROWNING

Gordon's child loose
between the old mare's hoofs
apparently invulnerable
The horse
sights along her flanks
considering
mouth trails
a sheaf of hay

the kind of summer day
when everything is waiting
lazily for movement

This mood broken
when his wife came up suddenly
from the house, waving a teatowel
yelled "someone fell in
the Kicking Horse River"

The mare jumped away mad
the child's laugh broke
to crying, we grabbed her up
and were off running

I cursed my riding boots
into running shoes
down that highway
the light flashing
Gordon swore once
at the crawling trailers

Then down the big hill,
where blasted walls
of limestone
sometimes block the traffic
with rockfalls
delays the smearing
of lesser mammals

Down to the whirlpool
under the bridge
where bovine tourists
gawk, and fool with zoom lenses

Ten minutes gone
and it's no use
but we hop and skip
down the cruel rocks

Below the arches
a sheer drop
His brother
saw him fall there
said he didn't come up

His brother dazed
and white
relates the story
over and over
Knowing he
must tell it to himself
for many years
Must get it right

2.

The Kicking Horse River
conceived from glaciers
of the Great Divide
weaves all its threads
July increased
in a deep sweet pool

Lake Wapta
thrusts it down the gorge
a river

Under the new road
frost heaved
through steel tubes
high as a man
and down to Field,
the rocks roll unseen
in a savage twist
of white and green

So we looked for him
snagged on struts
hooked on gaunt
pine trunks
Crushed and held
in rolling boulders
to set him free

Then the boat went in
the backwater
Moving around the sad pool
they grappled him

He rose in the boat's lee
dully shining
man from the water
hair floating backwards

They dragged him out
past the tunnel's
gaping trap
giving that some thought

We laid him down, open eyed
pain of this world on his face
Grief struck, surprised
to find the end of his life

On the brink
stood the curious
with their cameras
and with cameras
their wives

ON THE BOUNDARY

One day we packed to go together
patrolling the boundary
in soaking rains, chill September

It is hunting season
and poachers eye their maps
in towns beyond the mountains
I was a green pin they moved
predictable target

Through the contour lines
they zero in
get me out of focus against the taiga
my naked head grows horns

Last year a guide and his yankee hunters
threatened a warden with loaded rifles

Tie the 270
beneath the stirrup
carefully, and tonight
I'll have blistered knees

Dejected, the horses
grunt with their loads
seeing the corral now closed
follow without much cursing

We ride forward toward the Rocky River
talking of hunters
and women we once knew

ROUTINE

Moose runs out from the salt lick
as I amble toward the corral
a great silent shadow
with a silver tree for a head

Yesterday, he put the run on the woman
when she raised her voice to him
and when she retreated giggling
behind a tree
he thought this mockery of his bent face
and leaped, standing, over a four foot fence
graceful as a giant gazelle

I almost catch his scent
as he waits upwind
graciously
while I piss beside the manger
talking to the mare
who expertly blocks the gelding
from getting his share of the hay
by laying back her ears
and shifting her hind legs
threateningly towards him

The mare's in heat
and though she kicks and nips him daily
the gelding's revenge is poetic
So unfair, that I consider
planting a salt block
inside the corral

That old six pointer
might just bust in here
cover the mare for us
in the process of being
worth his salt

It would be
a cheap thrill for me
breaking my routine
to see a wild Canadian beast
domesticated so
(moose moving closer now)
pausing at my growing
man made salt lick, which
hey!
might be dangerous
for me too, come to think of it

TO A BLACK BEAR

It was a boring day
you wanted some fun
so chased the boss's wife
into her log kitchen
clawed some paint off the door
to hear her howl

Petulant
you wandered about our yard
hidden in willows

I baited the culvert trap
with rotten sardines
you feigned indifference

I had plans for you
A change of scene,
new country
without women to entertain

Sulking
you sniffed around
a squirrel's cache
I went to my trailer
to get some old wieners

With the same idea
unmindful of each other
we arrived, me at my front door
you ambling in the open rear
into my bedroom

We met in the kitchen

"Woof" you said
startled while trying the fridge
I forget what I said,
Your black fur made quite a contrast
against that white porcelain

Being both timid
we turned simultaneously
and attempted to exit
in embarrassed haste

The shiny linoleum
froze the action
I slipped and fell,
your claws lost traction

I made it at length
You shouldered through back there
wiped out two metal doors
with a fine backhand
carried them off
like streamers of tinfoil

Forgive me
in consternation,
I spoke rashly, obscene
loaded the shotgun

Boring days will never come again
to this sleepy warden station

IN THIS SEASON

In this season
between spring and summer
the lake hangs
at the end of the clearing
a green blaze
the moon stands in it
a sky tilted

I travel the mountain road
with my wounded
downhill moon of love

The North Star, Venus
at extremities
The night is full of bird song,
But today two grizzly bears
fought to the death west of here
in the wide daylight
and one is dead
with the moon in his eyes,
his heart is open now

I come to you, try to be gentle
Brother is set on brother
but I will keep beside you
of all others

Down this road, scent of iron and oil
Voices on the radio
They say two bears west of here
fighting by the Yellowhead road

Step on the gas. . . .
All these dark trees
this rock and water
unrelieved

And somewhere east of here
you wait
for this gold moon
my love

DEER LODGE, OFF SEASON *(for Andy)*

I'm here to stand
quietly now
Where I once swam up
the moonlit road at bay
When I was the warden
at Takkakaw Falls
and heard that water
Falling all the day

The fierce river at my cabin steps
That first threatened, and later
Bore me away, each night asleep
Rocking me under

I'd come in the night to my friend
In the midst of pressing his poems
On mulberry sheets, that looked
Like the woodchips from my axe

Having rested the bones of trees
With runes graven on cirque walls
He got out his bottles, the liquid
Brought forth swimming maidens

We drowned each one carefully
Twining rainbow trout and salmon
In their hair of black or golden
Then rescued them all, before

They floated into the world
And over Takkakaw Falls
That I might sleep
In the mountain night
Not to be out with the lantern
Scaring my horses with light

I'm here to stand quietly now
The first November avalanche
On Mount Victoria so far away
Breaks like a page
from this blue story
Into the legends of Abbot's Pass

FINDING A WOMAN

With a woman you begin
and find an end
within a limit that expands
taking your measure

A woman rocks you, vessel and home
not yours, your gift is only a birthright
your worth is not assured

Trying his limits, a man grows
to fit a vessel, his measure taken
within a limit that expands
to all of sea-room
rocking in the night

A woman you touch from the inside
touching of an oyster and a pearl
touching of your own skin
making sure she's really there
not you, but around you
Within the compass of waters
you must shine
and be home

Compression is the force
to carry the ocean
against your centre

hove to on blood
in an anchoring ground
It makes your measure
an element that is a harbour

a woman you live with
touching her, seeing her
for a place to sail the words
in senses
you can only trust to depth

Delights unfathomable
of the volatile medium
So many lifetimes
that can't be lived

so many lines cast out
cut adrift, returning
to the same waters

As willow wands bend for a well
is finding a woman
Losing, to be
deadwood
in a seachange

Leaving a woman
a loss of boundary
and finding a woman
an expansion, a surrender

SHE ASKS FOR A HISTORY

It began as a stallion with a mare
begins on a cold mountain night
where we tumble in blankets
in summer mountains, the nights are cold
clouds come in over the moon,
there will be snow

The fire of it
when outside us
the alien air waits
for an opening,
for the covers to slip
to the floor

Then you took your own shape
filled other spaces
lover, companion
who dawdles, picking blue berries
with a blue tongue,
the different berries
that grow here
while crying out at flowers
and tracks of animals,
your mouth
my only berry

Now your life cannot be
circumscribed by me
For the compass foot wavers
to the wild borealis
And you are alone
in the patch of berries
The forest has many ears
stealing your voice in hollows
to carry it understone

Now it's I must wait for you
In agony of the precision
your figure traces on the sun,
In pain with the distance
skin no longer heals

To see your image lashed
by rock and limb
to know a separation
troubling me

I hold you too tightly now
gaze too earnestly into your eyes
in my selfishness, my unmanly fear

We are so naked
when the covers
slip to the floor

DEPARTURE

Now we have pushed those boundaries
those edgings
on the maps of skin
"fallings from us, vanishings"
all out
from the real tone
of things

And the old questions
are still unanswered
What is true?
and believable, therefore

Wordsworth's sexless decay,
Sartre's black trees
or the red wing tips
of this flying whorehouse
I ride in,
bound for an old world

I tell you
I have climbed mountains
But what are they

What are they
but blue skies driven crazy cornered
sharpened
by the weight of heavy resolutions
in which we played no part

But they
are the headlong ships of my blood
sailing through a land
of animals and flowers
sailing through me
A man

Sept. 1971

THE BLAZE

This scar on the pine tree
is choked with pitch
the hairs of a bear
that brushed by
with crystals of heavy dew
stuck there

This wound that is my guide
is nearly healed
marks the journey
begun by other men
isolated, on lonely missions

Over the years
each made his mark
as I do now

Some got lost
in the green offing
whose loss added to our knowledge
We who remain to continue the journey

Laura, this creek is called
for one of their women

Happy, unhappy name
we know not
There is no record
The route not old enough
for history, not new enough
for memory
is but a weave
in a canyon

We who continue, maintain
our own winding stories
in this name

THE DEATH OF MUSTAHYAH

The big silvertip grizzly
Who fearsomely lived
red eyed and tough
by Moosehorn Lakes
is dead

The bear who left his claw marks
white on the bleeding spruce
by the windswept water
Who fed on squirrels, lambs
beetles and dead horses
whose scent was a presence
on the wind, who chased his sows
for hours through the avalanche slopes
and mated secretly in the thickets
making the mountains ring with the battle
is dead

His terrible hide is a rag
in a rich man's fist
his lard sticks in the raven's craw

He was shot out of season
by a poaching guide
for yankee dollars

He was sold to the highest bidder
as a fixture in this sold out land
His skeleton stinks
an extant document of corruption

Having killed his sons
his seed is nullified

Now the lake is tame, sullen
the only thing that moves in the wind
is Kakakew, the greasy raven

June 1972
Moosehorn Valley

LIGHTNING STORM

The forestry line is shorted out
has been for weeks
Picking up the ear piece
we hear
a thousand birds on a wire
miles apart
each in separate song
I don't know how this can be
While somewhere a lynx growls
from a lodgepole pine
where a bird was singing
on an insulator

During the lightning storm
the bell rings slowly
on every strike
resistors smoke
the line to Jasper is out
The district warden's 30 miles up
the Little Cairn river
hasn't been heard from
can't be reached

Twelve spruce have fallen
on the lines at Beaver Cabin
In the morning, we'll be climbing
splicing wire, cutting deadfalls
with the chainsaw

Answering the switchboard's ring
I shout, "do you need help?"
Far away the faint voice
fades in the sound of lightning
sound of wild cats in the timber

CAIRN PASS *(Jasper Park)*

On horse, Cairn Pass
and losing time
chasing a gone pony
through the deer yards
The mare sidesteps old antlers
Earth claws for me,
come down young lover

The lightning storm
will catch me at the summit
this wild bitch fighting the halter
take a dally round the saddle horn
My reluctant filly
drag you home

Sing of Big Lonely
shout into the drizzle
as it were a black wing
rains poison on
the soul beneath

Rocks fall
shotgun of Cairn Mountain
cross my path
when the big fingers
stab up high
Electric chorus lays it on

A young ram posed
in the black shales yesterday
Now the wild flowers
are deserts of winter

This the first storm of that season
broods on, freezes my intrusions
Its searching fingers nip my groin
wet and icy where the old chaps end

Wish I felt some warm hands now
woman bringing coffee in
lazing in bed, and home with love

PURPLE

When you are lying lovely
sure of every angle
in winter's rough couch

a shaft of snow
married to rock
where deep purple
crowns the pole star

shift the field
your eyes turn the distance
this camp of hanging valleys
days unseen by men

and smile
as falling mountains
slowly change
breaking themselves
to shake the world

Love's giant life,

shake me

FIVE WOLVES

Five wolves roll by Summit Lake
in the yellow grass
wrapped in the blood of a cow moose
spread by the shore

Ravens rise like smoke
whistling dipthong
croaking

These marrowbones are rich, elastic
The tracks tell of a sudden ambush
Mooshwa driven by dog wolf
out of the timber, cut down in the open
inches from safe water by the bitch
and the savaging pups, hamstrung
now nothing but hooves and hair
All else in the wolve's belly
in a black bear that fed
and coyote, sneaking in for a quick bite

2.

This was always wolf country
In the mornings they laughed around me
in the mists, as I jingled horses
their hunting songs far off, then suddenly near
on the trail far from home
that and the bugling elk bulls
I most recall
of autumn, the stirring air

Their curiosity's well known
and I have seen their tracks
on my backtrail, seen where they've watched
while I sat smoking

An old mountain man tells
of how they treed him
stalked him through the snow
Told of dropping branches
in a pile, dropping sparks
from his fire-bag
to burn himself free
of their wavering interest
If he was afraid, he didn't say

Lord Southesk, first traveller
in these ranges, admits no fear

In 1859 he wrote
  "While coming home, I saw
    an old wolf a long way off
and saluted him, with both barrels"

travelling for his health and pleasure

  "sat up late, reading much ado
    about nothing . . . the wolves howled
    the night was very cold"

and a white wolf chased his dog
back into camp, in the wilderness

RIDING OUT OF ROCKY FORKS COUNTRY

Ten days on the boundary
the black mare's knees swell up
erupt in yellow pus
so it's decided to bring her out
through Cairn Pass
down the river, the Medicine Tent

From the outpost Grizzly Shelter
a trail runs through willow, through alder
by the river, and rich soapberries
good bearfood grow there

Rode singing in a light rain

There was bearshit, full of red berries
track of the little stocky brown
three or four years old, and has
a cinnamon mantle
to his thickset shoulders

Ranging the valleys, he's wild
disdaining the highway
he combs the sidehills
strong as a young spruce, fat
with pounds of wintering lard

These scats are fresh
the tracks ooze water
as he prowls ahead of me
and once he barks beside me
somewhere in a dogwood thicket
The horses ears swivel slowly
trained on him like radar cones

Keep moving little brother
I say, to let him know who's coming
It is he
I smell his rank musk
and he knows my voice
of old

Don't mess with us
I tell him
This black mare kicks like thunder
poor little bear
and with my axe
I'd split your skull
should you choose to close
this distance, clearly
we have you outnumbered
I tell him, and I know

There is no fear to smell on me
ten days horse sweat and stiff jeans
that stand up by themselves

But it's not love that makes me sing
though little bear offers no trouble

His presence makes me cunning
cold with a cold rain
and quick moving

I will sing my song for him
and this weather

Brother, we will travel together
deadheading down, unseen to each other
as you lead me to the road

Brother, we will sound each other
when the wind shifts

We shall be certain
of one another
brother bear

COYOTE AGAIN

Coyote keeps his real name secret
so no one gets that handle to beat him with

He's seen Mustahyah rubbed out
and offered a bowl of his own liver
in tribute from his killers

Mustahyah skinned out
looking like a heavy muscled man
with talons

Coyote's flesh is ranker than a carcajou's
His hide is full of fleas
Even a starving Methodist missionary
spurned the flesh of the yellow dog

Coyote pisses on the strychnine baits
to warn off other creatures
He steals the bait from the leghold traps
and turns them over
He wrecks the snares set for Sehkos
the weasel, and sometimes gets caught
gets his head clubbed in

Returning in other pelts, he walks
over the graves of pious men
looking for secret vices

Goes on living, closer to the town
each year, until he winds up
feeding in the alleys of night
a jump away from the bush or prairie

Full of pride, he makes up melodies
to multiply his saga, a skilled ventriloquist
moving in from all directions at once

He sings, breeds gleefully
with any cur he finds
and prospers accordingly

He eats whatever he runs down
He eats the afterbirth of the deer
He eats shit when times are hard
or tells fortunes from it with his nose

He eats the bones of Mustahyah
thrown on the dungheap behind the corral

PUSHING THE BOUNDARY

On the boundary
the crossfire world
bends from the foothills
the prairie
out where they hunt
with impunity
Taking their guns
from jewelled scabbards
sighting into the sky

In here we declare
only the animals
may kill each other
sometimes
may even kill us

But it's hard to draw
the boundary
imaginary line
that cuts the watersheds
You got to know the ground
climb the crumbling mountain walls
to know which way the rivers run
headwaters, where the world begins

Magic bullets
sing straight
through any flesh
weighted with ink to paper

The Big Horn Rams
dragging their broken
hindquarters
over the finish line
do not believe it
seeing my revolver

Of square miles
I've a thousand to cover

Like a wolf on the prowl
I leave tracks in the passes
so the killers will know
there's a killer riding the boundary

My markers at various places
I often find riddled with bullets
but I smile
the shots come from outside

And dressed all in green
I float among the trees
Staring out on the plains
in September
to hear the distant roll of guns
draw near

INVITATION AND COVENANT

Yet you are alone with me
even in the arms of my daughters
and now, when fantasies of night
loom up
as the sharp hands of mountains

Come out
from all that ordering geometry
Unlatch the cabin door, forget
the tales of being bushed
for you
are far beyond them,
I promise you

I promise you
the cold starlight
of October

The frost on the willow
to rouse your naked foot

With the feel of my breath
upon your loins
like a glacier
birthing in your blood

Though you see
nothing of me,
turn your back
on the golden door

Forget the stories
forget geometry

It was a night in October
far up the Moosehorn Valley
Now it is the moon of frozen leaves
You are alone
(it is beginning to snow

Oct./Nov. 1972